DESIGN & DRAW
50 CAT OUTFITS

T0088735

Illustrated by Christine Sheldon
Text by Elizabeth Golding
Designed by Anton Poitier and Becca Wildman

About This Book

There are 50 cats and kittens to dress in this book! Each of them has a job or hobby to give you a clue about what they might wear. Use colored pencils or felt-tip pens to fill in the missing parts with fabulous fashion. If you need inspiration, there are lots of ideas at the end of the book.

Have fun!

Copyright © 2021 iSeek Ltd.

ISBN: 978-1-64722-311-3

This book was conceived, created, and produced by iSeek Ltd.
an imprint of Insight Editions

www.insightseditions.com

Insight Editions PO Box 3088 San Rafael, CA 94912

Printed in China

10 9 8 7 6 5 4 3 2 1

All rights reserved. No part of this publication may be copied, reproduced, or transmitted in any form or by any means, without permission of the publishers.

Practice with me!
I'd like a pretty dress
with spots, please!

I'm a gymnast!

I'm a chef!

I'd like a dress and red bow, please!

I like shopping!

I'm a zookeeper!

I ride horses!

I like to go fishing!

I play soccer!

I'm a spy!

I'm an Arctic explorer!

I work in a library!

I'm a gardener!

We are nurses!

Dress me up as a monster!

I am a firefighter!

I like running!

I like to jump!

I like cooking!

Make me a queen!

Make me a king!

I'm a vet!

We like to go swimming!

I'm a carpenter!

I am a race car driver!

Dress us up as unicorns!

We would like flowery hats, please!

I am a pop star!

I can do handstands!

Let's chase butterflies!

I like to skateboard!

Dress me up as an alien!

I am a scientist!

I'm a teacher!

We are detectives!

I make cookies!

I'd like a top hat, please!

Dress me up as a mermaid!

I am a fashion designer!

We like making lemonade!

I'm a baker!

I am a sea captain!

We are helicopter pilots!

I like shoes!

Helpful tips!

Dark blue would look good on this jacket.

A long trench coat would be a good look for me!

I'm an Arctic explorer!
A pink top and red skirt might suit me!

I like to wear checkered vests.
We are nurses!

Dress me up as a monster!
I am a firefighter!
I would wear my running number on my shirt!
1

I like to jump!
Dark blue spots look nice on a light blue background!

Dress me in royal colors!

Stripes always look good on swimwear!
I'm a vet!

I'm a carpenter!
I am a race car driver!
Pastel colors would look nice on us!

Add flowers!
We would like flowery hats, please!
Dress me all in black!

I can do handstands!
I think a blue shirt would look cool!

I like to skateboard!
Dress me up as an alien!
Draw a long lab coat on me!

I'm a teacher!
1 2 3
4 5 6
7 8 9
Blue coats could disguise us well!
We want to be detectives!

I make cookies!
I'd like a top hat, please!
You could give me a teal and purple tail!

We like making lemonade!
Pink and red go together nicely!

Give us flying outfits!

A red dress goes with all of these shoes!